THE TRUCKS OF THE TRANS PENNINE RUN

A Photographic History

Roy Dodsworth

Old Pond PUBLISHING

First published 2016

Copyright © Roy Dodsworth 2016

Published by
Old Pond Publishing,
An imprint of 5M Publishing Ltd,
Benchmark House,
8 Smithy Wood Drive,
Sheffield, S35 1QN, UK
Tel: +44 (0) 0114 246 4799
www.oldpond.com

A catalogue record for this book is available from the British Library

ISBN 978-1-910456-50-7

Book layout by Servis Filmsetting Ltd, Stockport, Cheshire
Printed by Replika Press Pvt Ltd, India
Photos by Roy Dodsworth, unless otherwise indicated

Contents

Preface

In 1968 the first Trans Pennine Run took place, and as always the date was fixed for the first Sunday in August.

It was organised by three enthusiasts who were members of the Historic Commercial Vehicle Club, North Midlands (now Society – HCVS Yorkshire region).

The club organises the annual London to Brighton Run for commercial vehicles, and it was thought that a run should be organised north of Watford Gap.

The organisers – two lived in Lancashire, one in Yorkshire – decided to create an event that would link both sides of the Pennines and, as a bonus, travel through the beautiful scenery of the Pennines.

A start at Manchester and a finish in Harrogate was decided and the mammoth task of putting everything in place was commenced.

Following negotiations with Manchester City FC, permission was granted for the use of its car park at Maine Road, while at Harrogate the council enthusiastically agreed to allow the use of their car park adjacent to the Royal Hall/Exhibition Centre as the finishing point.

It was felt that a refreshment stop was needed somewhere along the 64-mile route, and the world-famous Harry Ramsden's fish and chip restaurant at Guiseley kindly agreed to the use of their car park for this purpose. This has now changed hands, and all entrants stop as and when necessary.

In the late 1990s I used to sit there, eating fish and chips, and watch all the entrants pass by. I would then go to The Stray at Harrogate and take photographs, amassing a collection of over 3000.

The success of the first run ensured that it has been repeated every year since. The main change at the Harrogate end is that the finishing point has moved to The Stray, although on occasion, due to weather, the location has moved to the grounds of a local college.

The start has been moved several times, including to Salford University (1971), Belle Vue Manchester (1972 to 1978), GMT buses Hyde Road garage (1978 to 1988), ADT auction centre (1989 and 1990), Astley Green Colliery Museum (1991 to 1999), Popular Truck Stop at Lymm (2000 and 2001) and then Birch Motorway Services M62 from 2002 to present.

The finish was held at Royal Hall Car Park and Exhibition Centre Harrogate from 1969 to 1972. In 1973 it was at The Stray, Knaresborough Road, Harrogate, moving to its current position in 1974.

The run organisation starts a few weeks after the last event ended. A small committee exists, and the events are well attended by entrants and spectators. Every year each entrant receives a souvenir of that year's event: sadly due to expense, plaques are no longer given, but a vehicle display notice, showing entry number, is issued for attaching to each vehicle. Prizes are given for winners in various categories. The once renowned colour programmes have given way to a less costly black and white run guide.

Entry to the run has attracted additional features, and two of the most appreciated include the recovery service provided by Highway Recovery for any vehicle in distress. Their vehicle travels the route after the last entrant has left Birch Services. Thankfully most runs are trouble free.

The other feature is the two packed lunches each entrant gets at lunchtime at Harrogate. These have kindly been prepared and distributed by Huntapac Produce. The owners, the Hunter family, also enter a number of vehicles from their classic truck collection.

This event can only continue thanks to a dedicated team of enthusiasts who work hard all year to ensure a smooth-running event, the enthusiasts who enter their vehicles, and the spectators who attend.

I hope you enjoy this book. It has been difficult selecting photographs of the vehicles that appear, although I think there is a good selection of trucks in the categories entered. Although the event is open to all types of vehicle, this book concentrates on trucks only.

ROY DODSWORTH

RECOMMENDED TRANS PENNINE ROUTE

En Route

The trip across the Pennines is a great event in the lives of many of the old vehicles which will be taking part in the run today. Each vehicle will carry an entry number to enable you to easily find its details in the programme.

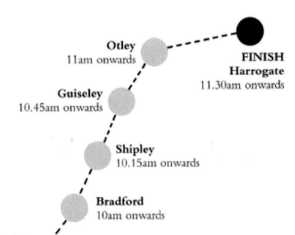

Otley
11am onwards

FINISH
Harrogate
11.30am onwards

Guiseley
10.45am onwards

Shipley
10.15am onwards

Bradford
10am onwards

Shelf
9.45am onwards

Halifax
9.15am onwards

At Harrogate

Whilst we invite you to inspect all the wonderful old and not so old vehicles on display, we ask that you wait until they are parked. If you want to look inside any of them please remember to ask the owners first. If you want to know any more, you will find their owners or drivers generally very keen to talk about their vehicles.

Toilet facilities are available at the Knaresborough Road end of the site. Refreshments and ice creams are available in the display area.

Please ...

Do be careful - lorries and buses are big and can be dangerous when moving.

Don't leave litter - use bins provided.

Todmorden
8.45am onwards

Rochdale
8.15am onwards

START
BIRCH SERVICES, MIDDLETON
From 7.30am

A map of the route.

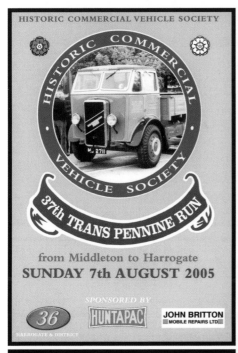

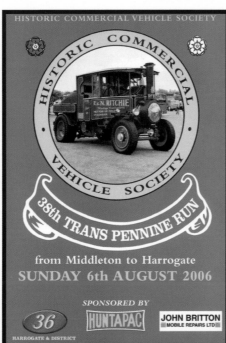

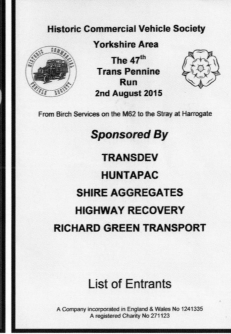

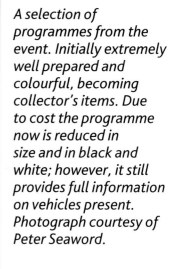

A selection of programmes from the event. Initially extremely well prepared and colourful, becoming collector's items. Due to cost the programme now is reduced in size and in black and white; however, it still provides full information on vehicles present. Photograph courtesy of Peter Seaword.

A selection of plaques issued in recent years. These were given to vehicle owners on arrival at the finish at Harrogate. It is not unusual to see vehicles displayed with a board containing numerous plaques collected over the years. Photograph courtesy of Peter Seaword.

The start of the book and the start of the run at Birch Services M62. This picture was taken at 0630 in 2010. I start taking photographs as vehicles arrive, assisting with marshalling as necessary. On arrival, drivers check in, get any route changes, and a windscreen banner giving entry details. Set-off time is 0800. I then drive to the finish at The Stray, Harrogate, taking further pictures as vehicles arrive. The taxi seen leaving is a 1935 Austin 12/4 taxicab. The route starts in Greater Manchester and passes through West Yorkshire, ending in North Yorkshire.

A 1960 Thornycroft Trident delivery van, fitted with a CR6/1 engine. Fleet number 56 and used by Timothy White & Taylors, a once famous high street retailer. It entered a number of Trans Pennine rallies in the early years of the millennium but was not seen again for some time. Some two weeks after writing this caption I saw an advert in a truck magazine with the following information: 'For sale £18,500 ono. £1000s spent on a long restoration 20 years ago. Laid up for last ten years but started regularly. Some history. Original maintenance manual.' So with luck we may see it on a rally some time?

Roy Dodsworth collection 2002

This is a 1946 Citroen U23 type R. It has a two-litre OHV engine and a four-speed crash gearbox. Bought off French eBay in 2007, it had not run since 1966 and had only 64,000 kilometres on the clock. It was previously owned by L. & H. Taffit et Fils of Charente, the Cognac region. The restoration took 18 months and it was first shown at the NEC Classic car show in 2008. I have not seen it since.

Roy Dodsworth collection

Here is a 1962 Rowe Hillmaster, one of a limited quantity built by a bus operator in Cornwall. This is in the livery of Colin Pitt, a commercial vehicle restorer from Otley. It was repainted in his name with a green livery, and was later sold to a buyer in Northern Ireland. A small number of trucks were made, together with a bus chassis.

Another Rowe Hillmaster, built in 1957 as a box van for the Bank of England print works in Essex. Banknote paper is obviously a valuable commodity and in view of this the vehicle was fitted with toughened glass, security locks and a reinforced cab to protect the three-man crew. When disposed of, the body, heavily reinforced, was retained by the bank. Now fitted out as a chassis and cab.

A 1937 Albion truck, bought new by E. Sibley, a coal merchant from Southampton. It has entered the Trans Pennine on a number of occasions, whilst still a working lorry. Seen here in 1997 loaded with Monday's delivery. Loaded up on Saturday, enter rally Sunday, and then deliver Monday. Whereabouts not now known.

A 1913 Thornycroft ST model, 30 cwt light truck, new to Hull Corporation and sold in 1920 to Drypool Engineering. Is the oldest-known, still-running Thornycroft with a petrol engine. This vehicle was the first one made and is one of a range of worm-drive types replacing the earlier range of chain-drive vehicles. When new it was fitted with an engine of 3.47 litres, and four cylinders; however, when found, the engine and gearbox were missing. Finding an engine and gearbox of the original type proved impossible. Luckily a four-litre unit and gearbox of 1930s vintage was found in a field in County Durham. This was refurbished and is now fitted. Originally it was fitted with a water tank and was used to spray water to lay the dust on the city's streets. Special permission was given by Hull City Council to use the corporate livery on restoration. Seen on a number of rallies annually and owned by Les Wilson of Harrogate.

A Ford D series two-axle flat truck, new to ICI Teesside in 1972 as a decontamination unit. Disposed of, and first registered in 1980. Now in the livery of Vaux Brewery, formerly of Sunderland and since closed down.

A 1973 AEC Mammoth Major eight-wheeled milk tanker, in the livery of Longley Farm, and owned by J. & E. Dickinson of Holmfirth. Restored by John Murphy from Huddersfield. AEC were part of Leyland Motors and this type of vehicle can be seen badged as a Leyland Octopus, fitted with an ERGO cab.

A 1927 Albion flatbed truck in the livery of Lyons' Cocoa (headboard) and Lyons' Tea on doors. Seen once at Harrogate and a couple of sightings on the London to Brighton truck run. Thought to have been restored by Andy Gibb, who has worked his wonders on other Albion vehicles.

Roy Dodsworth collect

Albion 355 flat truck seen climbing up Hollins Hill leading to a refreshment stop at Harry Ramsden's fish and chip shop at Guiseley. Seen in Livery of F. Richardson, Cabinetmakers, as 'Old Fred'. Also seen prior in the livery of J. Arnold & Sons of Eccleshall, Staffs. The insignia on the radiator translates as 'Sure as the sunrise' – a slogan emphasising reliability.

Roy Dodsworth collection.

This is a 1948 Bedford OB tractor unit coupled to a Scammell coupling trailer, seen at Harrogate in the livery of W. M. Burr of Ackworth. Later sold and now in the livery of Wynn's Haulage, it was seen for sale in October 2015. The vehicle was first registered to Robson's Malt Kilns of Pontefract.

A 1932 Bedford WS flat truck climbing Hollins Hill towards Guiseley. This is a publicity vehicle in the livery of Tennent's, a Scottish brewer. The company was known as Chevrolet Bedford when production first started. It is probably powered by a Chevrolet engine, which was well ahead of its time.

Roy Dodsworth collection.

A 1965 Bedford RL 4x4 recovery truck, ex-military, seen waiting for the off at Birch for the run to Harrogate. The RL was developed for military use and was popular with the British Army. The RL formed the basis of a Green Goddess, the fire tender designed for use during the cold war and used by the AFS.

T. & G. FOX

EYX 303C

Here we have a Commer QX Mk111 interim model four-wheeled drop-side truck, on the familiar route up Hollins Hill heading for Guiseley. In the livery of Ken Thomas, a transport company who have a number of restored trucks. This vehicle would be powered by a TS3 two-stroke engine. It has a characteristic noise and is easily identified by Commer enthusiasts. The later TS4 engine had four cylinders.

A 1945 Diamond T recovery truck in the livery of Hudson of Milnthorpe, Cumbria. Supplied new to the British Army in WW2 and used for tank movements. Following army release it was used for heavy recovery on the A6 over Shap Fell until 1997. Seen photographed in a yard at Greenodd but a frequent attender on the Trans Pennine, entered by M. Gregory.

A 1956 Dennis Pax flat truck, fitted with a Perkins diesel engine. Seen in the livery of Deighton Bros of Gateshead, Tyne and Wear. Dennis, whose vehicles are manufactured at Guildford in Surrey, have always marketed vehicles for municipal use and this continues.

A 1968 ERF LV tractor unit, fitted with a Gardner diesel engine, in the livery of Ribble Cement. Sometimes seen with a bulk cement tanker, it was restored by John Murphy of Huddersfield. ERF no longer exist: in financial difficulties, the company was bought by Man Truck and Bus who eventually shut the factory down.

Roy Dodsworth collection

A 1940 Bedford OXD 30 cwt truck owned by Mike Shackleton. It is a rare vehicle, with only three or four known to exist. It was found in a scrapyard in 1984 then restored and has been owned by Mike since 2011. Bedford manufactured approximately 24,500 vehicles for war service and they are favourites for preservation.

In 1939 when the country was on war alert Bedford quickly adapted their existing range to produce vehicles suitable for the War Department. This Bedford OVD series three-tonner General Service truck was one of the first, and during hostilities it is known to have served on the Eastern Front. No information of the restoration is known.

Roy Dodsworth collection.

A 1936 Fordson E88W 25 cwt truck. Seen at Harrogate 2009, this was a rare sighting of the Fordson model, and was in excellent condition. Fitted with a V8 2295 cc engine. This vehicle is bonneted and later models had larger headlights fitted on the wings, as seen here.

A 1957 Thames Trader new to Tom Maughan, now restored in the livery of Wynnstay animal feed supplier, and seen at Harrogate. The first truck to be designed by Ford of Dagenham, it appeared in two versions. This is a mark two version, as the word Thames appears on the engine cowl, with the word Trader on the radiator grille.

A 1957 Guy Invincible, fitted with a Willenhall cab. New to Ripponden and District Transport, a parcel carrier and operator of local buses in the Ripponden area. It worked for them with a drawbar trailer for ten years, and was used as a snow plough for the next 30 years. Acquired by the present owner, who gave it a total strip-down rebuild, with a rebuilt cab. Now fitted with a Gardner 6LW diesel engine and a David Brown five-speed gearbox.

Roy Dodsworth collection

A 1951 Guy Otter, restored in the livery of Silentnight, a manufacturer of mattresses, of Barnoldswick, Lancashire. Seen at the start point at Birch, and entered by Paul Sweeting. Guy were very successful with sales and offered a wide range of vehicles from four to eight wheels. The mascot on the radiator is of a North American Indian in full headgear. Due to financial difficulties the company was bought by Sir William Lyons of Jaguar fame and became part of BMC. The company disappeared in British Leyland days.

A 1963 Atkinson mark one two-axle tractor unit seen coupled to an unusually small tanker, and I do not know what the tanker carried. The vehicle has been restored in the livery of R. W. Morris, of Tarleton, and this was one of its first outings in 2011 when at Harrogate. Seen advertised for sale by 'Paul' on the Internet in 2012.

Magnet for Me is a strapline of John Smith's Brewery of Tadcaster, North Yorkshire, whose ales are still enjoyed in the North. Pictured here is an Atkinson F740HLA model, two-axle brewers dray. With a typical dray body fitted with chains, it is fleet numbered 102. Note the Magnet logo on the grille.

Roy Dodsworth collection

A 1962 Karrier Bantam mark five tipper. New to Walshaw & Drake Ltd, it was restored by two former employees. It is seen at Birch shortly before set-off for Harrogate. The company are still in business at Bradford as cloth dyers. West Yorkshire County Council bought quite a number of these vehicles, which were seen on highway repair work.

A 1991 photograph of a 1935 Leyland Beaver flat truck. It is fitted with a living-accommodation body and is in the livery of P. J. Boughey. A typical Leyland truck with solid looks. Leyland used a number of animal names, such as Bison, Buffalo, Beaver, Bull, Octopus and Steer. Comet followed later.

Roy Dodsworth collection.

A 1939 Leyland Lynx in the livery of James C. Ashworth of Bradford. This vehicle was restored by Bill Reid. Ashworth's were main hauliers of International Tractors from the Idle factory to Doncaster. They also had a number of larger trucks, which were used for carrying bales of wool to the numerous mills in Bradford.

Roy Dodsworth collection.

A 1959 Leyland Steer. The two steering axles and single rear axle is known as a Chinese Six. The vehicle was new to London Carriers and since has been seen in the liveries of Morgan Wright, K. Williams and now J. Ford. Seen at Birch prior to set-off for Harrogate. A sister vehicle WVB888 can be seen in the next picture.

ROY DODSWORTH COLLECTION 2011

A 1959 Leyland Steer ex London Carriers, now in the livery of Morgan Wright. Seen on entry to Birch Services M62. This is registered as WVB888, a sister vehicle to WVB887 pictured above. Entered by Alan Wright.

A Commer TS3 is fitted with a three-cylinder two-stroke Rootes diesel engine, which has a familiar sound instantly recognised by truck enthusiasts, and this C-range TS model has such an engine. The model is identified by twin headlights and a four-slot radiator grille. All Commer cabs of this design were made by Sankey of Birmingham. It is owned and was restored by John Murphy of Huddersfield, who has worked his magic on a number of preserved commercials.

A 1950 Morris Commercial FV12 new to Wheelwright Bros of Halifax.
Morris Commercial were part of the Nuffield Group, having being
bought by William Morris, later Lord Nuffield.

Roy Dodsworth colle

Another Wheelwright vehicle, this is a 1946 Morris
Commercial CVF 13-5 drop-side truck, parked alongside
KNY295 at The Stray, Harrogate. Wheelwright's also
had a collection of vintage Land-Rovers, including a rare
estate version, which he regularly showed at Harrogate.

A MAN 4141 drop-side truck. Of interest, it was manufactured in Germany in 1954 and was first registered in the UK in 1984 with a no-age registration DSV155. Unusually it is a right-hand version and a rare vehicle with a bonnet. MAN trucks and buses are now regularly on our roads.

M·A·N
DIESEL
415

DSV 155

MAN 415L3
TYPE   4x2 Bonnetted Cab
BODY   Dropside
PAYLOAD   5 ton
GVW   8 ton

Roy Dodswor

KEVIN SIMPSON

KEVIN SIMPSON
DAIRYMAN
Fresh Dairy Produce

LSV 203

LSV 203

A 1949 Morris Commercial drop-side truck in the livery of and owned by Kevin Simpson, a dairyman. The no-age registration was issued in 1984. Seen on The Stray at Harrogate, this is an unusual colour of white, but, being owned by a milkman, I suppose it is appropriate!

A 1963 Scammell Highway tractor unit, new to Shell in 1963 to 1968, and purchased by the Davis Brothers. Totally rebuilt by them, the truck's Meadows engine was replaced with a Leyland 680. It appeared newly painted at the Scammell stand at the 2008 commercial vehicle show and was much admired. Entered by Parry Davis.

A rare 1926 Overland 20 cwt drop-side truck. First manufactured in America by Willys-Overland and seen on the way to Harrogate in 2009. In 2013 it was seen in the livery of Reginald Thomas. This particular vehicle was built in the Manchester area by Willys-Overland-Crossley. Vehicles bearing the Manchester name, and Crossley trucks, came from the same factory.

Roy Dodsworth collection

A rare vehicle, a Pattison light truck, manufactured from the running gear of a Ford Model T. These were trucks for light agricultural, market garden use or similar, made in the 1920s at a factory at Stanmore, near Watford. In the livery of Progressive Engineering, Manchester. Seen at Harrogate in 2004.

1940 Scammell rigid eight flat truck making its way up
Hollins Hill towards Guiseley en route to Harrogate.
Following on behind is an eight-wheeled Atkinson in
the livery of Ken Thomas. Scammell Motors built trucks
at Watford, and a number of rigid eight models are
in restoration. Eventually Scammell became part of
Leyland Motors and subsequently closed down.

Roy Dodsworth collection.

Roy Dodsworth collection.

1951 Scammell Scarab articulated in the livery of
British Railways. This is a three-wheeled vehicle
with a single front steering wheel. Bearing BR fleet
number HN6185N, it is a regular rally entrant and
is seen here at Harrogate in 2003. They were very
popular in their day for quick turnarounds and seen
at almost every major railway station. A successor
to the Scarab was the Townsman, which had a GRP
(glass reinforced plastic) cab.

1935 Scammell K20 rigid six truck. Named Demetrius, it is in the livery of Robert Wynn, a famous haulier in their day. A very impressive well-turned-out vehicle. The name Wynn was familiar due to their expertise in heavy haulage transport and abnormal-sized loads worldwide.

ROBERT WYNN & SONS LTD

CARDIFF - LONDON

SCAMMELL

DEMETRIUS

Scammell Six Wheeler

52

GARDNER

BLT 235

Roy Do

UOG 594H

Roy Dodsworth collection.

A rare Seddon diesel four-wheeler tanker, new to North West Water in 1969. Shortly after manufacture of this vehicle, Seddon merged with Atkinson to form Seddon Atkinson trucks. This picture was taken in the late 1990s and I have not seen the vehicle since. Over the years I have seen that a number of preserved vehicles have 'disappeared'. I wonder where they get to?

Personally owned by Tom Riding, albeit the vehicle is in his company livery. A 1939 Scammell rigid eight flat truck. New to Albright and Wilson of Widnes, it was purchased for £1600 (£88,000 at the time of writing). Most of its working life was spent hauling steel plate. Bought by Mr Riding in 1988, it has been extensively rebuilt. It is fitted with the last Gardner diesel engine made by the company.

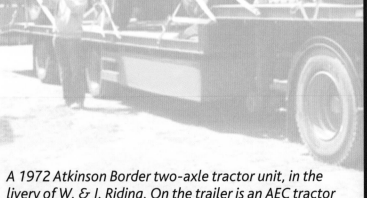

A 1972 Atkinson Border two-axle tractor unit, in the livery of W. & J. Riding. On the trailer is an AEC tractor unit and an ERGO-cabbed Leyland, AEC or Albion cab. W. & J. Riding are a long-established business in Lancashire. Tom Riding personally owns a Scammell eight-wheeler flat, seen in the previous image.

1950 Seddon mark five four-wheeled flat lorry, in the livery of and entered by Colin Pitt of Otley, a commercial vehicle restorer. Colin's fleet of restored vehicles are seen regularly at rallies throughout the season. This model is fitted with a Perkins diesel engine, and its first owner was Metal Box Company.

Roy Dodsworth collection

1970 Scammell Highwayman recovery vehicle in the livery of Bristow's Skip Hire. It has a Michelotti-designed cab and is seen at Harrogate. This vehicle probably started life as a tractor unit. The livery is easily recognised as that of Bristow's fleet.

Roy Dodsworth collection

Here we have a very rare vehicle, a 1926 Morris-Commercial one-ton T-type truck. Manufactured between 1924 and 1931, they cost £252/10 shillings when new. Unladen weight is 1461kg and the chassis number is 10958. It has a Hotchkiss-type four-cylinder engine 139 HP side-valve engine, foot and handbrake operated on drums to rear wheels only. Has also been seen with a canvas tilt.

A 1981 Bedford TK two-wheeler flat truck owned by John Tweedie of Skipton. On the front appears an Anglo Saxon maxim which when translated means 'Shame on whoever would think badly'. This is the motto of the Coldstream Guards, and the words appear in their insignia, so maybe John has some connection? Having names and mottos on preserved vehicles, and Stobart trucks, is quite common. Incidentally, when referring to a vehicle, invariably it is 'she'.

Roy Dodsworth collection 2009

Roy Dodsworth collection

A very rare imported 1919 Unic 10 truck, possibly the only one in the UK. Right-hand drive, new to Radcliffe Motor Contractor, London. Seen at the halfway halt at Guiseley in 2013. Unic trucks started business in 1905 in Paris and made a number of steam vehicles, moving on to cars and trucks. In 1938 car production stopped to concentrate on trucks. The company was taken over by Fiat in 1966 and in 1974 merged with Iveco.

Roy Dodsworth collection

A 1976 Volvo BX RH 33 four-wheeler in the livery of Ray Stephen of Stockton-on-Tees. Seen at Harry Ramsden's, Guiseley in 2003 on the way to Harrogate. This vehicle is a ballast tractor probably used for towing. Since launching in the UK, Volvo have been very successful with a huge modern range. They are also popular on the preserved scene.

A 1948 Guy Vixen in the livery of J. Leech of Haslington, Crewe. J. Leech have a number of classic commercials and are keen to exhibit at local rallies, so they are enthusiastic supporters of the Trans Pennine Run. Seen here travelling towards Harrogate, the Vixen cab was very similar to the Otter.

Roy Dodsworth collection 2002

A 1965 ERF KV four-wheeled drop-side truck. Again entered by J. Leech & Co. of Crewe and seen at Birch. The distinctive ERF factory-produced cab looks well in the familiar Leech livery.

Roy Dodsworth collection 2012

A 1984 Bedford TL two-axle rigid with a fitted horsebox body, in the striking livery of Bailey & Co., specialist equestrian removers. The vehicle is seen at Harrogate. It has been spotted at a number of rallies in 2015. The Bedford TL chassis was popular with specialist body builders. Smart varnished bodywork.

Roy Dodsworth collection 2015

A 1959 Dennis Pax fitted with a 4.5-litre diesel engine, used as a fuel tanker by Armer Fuels. This vehicle is a regular rally attender and pictured at Birch. The forward control model was a popular vehicle with municipal authorities. A left-hand-drive version often seen as a gully emptier.

A 1962 Ford Thames Trader 6D in the livery of Brandon & Son of Wigan. This was new to British Aerospace, Aircraft Group, of Weybridge, and used by them on airfield operations for de-icing. It was fitted with a 50-foot Simon hoist, but is now restored as a platform lorry. When sold to its second owner in 1995, the mileage was 4300, and still on original tyres. This is a mark one version, with 'Thames Trader' on the radiator grille.

This is a 1957 Atkinson 4A four-wheeled drop-side truck, built new for Nightingales, main Atkinson dealers of London, now in the livery of G. Preston. Fitted with a Gardner 6LW engine and a David Brown gearbox, and seen at Birch, this vehicle was built at Walton le Dale prior to the takeover by Seddon vehicles of Oldham.

A 1933 Manchester BX2 four-wheeled flat truck, chassis number MT30582, one of the last made before the company went into liquidation. In the livery of Lynch Truck Services of Accrington, and seen at Birch. Manchester trucks were built at Heaton Chapel, Stockport, a joint venture with Willys-Overland-Crossley. In 1928 the vehicle range was modified and the name Manchester adopted. Available with bodywork or as a rolling chassis.

A 1968 Commer C series four-wheeled flat truck, in the livery of Jim Ellis of Kendal. Seen at the start at Birch, it is fitted with a TS3 diesel engine, two stroke with three cylinders. When it is running, enthusiasts enjoy listening to the engine's distinctive tone. A development of the engine was a TS4 four cylinder. Part of the Rootes group, later merged with Dodge and finally Renault.

A 1986 Leyland Constructor six-wheeled flat truck in the livery of C. & W. Berry of Leyland. Seen carrying items of plant, this is a working vehicle in regular use. The Constructor took over from the Bison and Buffalo models. It used the T45 cab as seen on the Road Train. Most production was of six-wheeled vehicles, although eight-wheeled, and four- and six-wheeled tractor units were available.

A 1976 Foden S90, which the Army used as a medium-mobility tanker, fitted with a Motor Panels cab. Seen at the start at Birch. Foden, manufactured at Sandbach in Cheshire, were successful in gaining large military contracts. They were classed as low mobility, for use on normal roads, or high mobility, which were 6x6 or 24-ton 6x4 tankers, such as this, capable of negotiating cross-country terrain. A powerful-looking vehicle.

Roy Dodswor

An AEC 690 Dumptruck, model BDK6R, fitted with a ten-cubic-yard truck body, fleet number GW40. Four-by-four drive, the vehicle is in the familiar livery of Wimpey. This vehicle was designed by Thornycroft, which AEC took over in 1961. The engine was 150/192 HP, and was also badged as Aveling Barford. When Leyland took over, the engine was revamped to 160/265 HP.

A 1987 Freightliner six-wheeled-drive truck, fitted with a flat body and a loading crane to front. Made in the USA, left-hand drive and seen here at Birch. Freightliner is a member of Daimler Trucks' North American division, with headquarters in Oregon, USA. Over the years it has experienced labour and financial difficulties and now produces only specialised vehicles. Towards the end of the 1980s USA car and truck builders were involved in long union disputes, causing major cash loss and disruption.

A smart 1960 Bedford RL 4x4 fire tender. Body built by Firearmour, a one-off design, later taken over by HCB/Angus, and used at Oxford (Kidlington) Airport. The RL was the British Army medium truck. Built from the 1950s to late 1960s, it superseded the OY model. Rated at three tons, it was fitted with a 4.9-litre petrol engine.

Quite a rare vehicle, this is a 1961 Seddon DD8 eight-wheeled tipper, owned by Richardson's of Oldham. New as a bulk sugar discharger on contract from BRS to the British Sugar Corporation, Lincolnshire, it then passed into fairground work with G. Tuby of Doncaster. It was bought for preservation in 1995 and rebuilt as a tipper, fitted with Gardner 150 LX engine, David Brown five-speed gearbox, with overdrive, and Kirkstall axles.

This is a vehicle rarely seen in the UK: a 1963 Hanomag, type AL28, 4x4. It was used as a command centre by police on the border of East and West Germany. Hanomag started building steam vehicles and locomotives in the early 1900s. During WW2 they built over 15,000 troop carriers. After the war they continued building special vehicles, such as this, for the army and security services. The board at the front of the vehicle shows a number of attendance plaques given out at events.

POLIZEI ✠ ▮6740◉2B▮

Roy Dodsworth c

A 1950 Leyland Beaver tractor unit which tows an authentic pole truck as used by the firm of Arthur Green, Timber Merchant of Steeton, West Yorkshire. The vehicle was restored in the firm's livery in 1997 and is seen regularly at classic events up and down the country. It is owned by Richard Green, who along with others kindly sponsors Trans Pennine events. Despite its Cumbrian registration, the vehicle was new to Holmes of Preston, and later passed on to Codonas, who were showmen. When restored it was shortened to make a suitable tractor unit. Andrew Green is seen driving and Richard is the passenger.

This is a 1981 Scania LB 11 HS 34 tractor unit. New to Arthur Green Transport Ltd, Steeton, it is owned by Richard and Andrew Green, pictured in the previous picture. It was bought new and cost £24,265. It was used on international haulage for some time and has done high mileage. Together with the pole truck, this vehicle can be seen at many events during the season.

A 1969 AEC Mandator V8 2VT G4R4355 tractor unit, new to the Road Transport Institute Training Board and used for driver training. Associated Equipment Company (AEC) was taken over by Leyland in the early 1960s. Gradually all the group vehicles used a standard ERGO-style cab. Seen on The Stray.

Roy Dodsworth collection 2002

Not a classic commercial, but very worthy of a mention. As stated in the preface, Highway Recovery annually provide a recovery service, leaving Birch Services after the last vehicle has left, and dealing with any issues on the way. This is a DAF 95XF and the registration is of note: HR03DAF.

Roy Dodsworth collection 2002

This is an Albion KL26 four-wheeled truck, restored in the livery of Shell Mex and BP. Superbly finished, it creates a lot of interest. It was first registered on 1 May 1938, and has a 3950 cc petrol engine, being designated as a can carrier.

This is a Foden S series manufactured in 1934 and restored from 'bits' in 1998, the rebuild taking six years. One of two classic trucks owned by John O'Shaughnessey of Huddersfield, it is seen at Birch, only a few miles from home, ready for the off to Harrogate. This S series truck is a rare example of the marque, with very few in preservation.

A 1971 Albion Chieftain in the livery of J. Leech & Co. of Crewe. The vehicle has a box body recovered from an ex Ripponden and District vehicle, all of which had a distinctive body, and has the familiar LAD cab. Entered by James Leech.

A 1971 Atkinson Silver Knight eight wheeler, with twin-wheel rear axles. It is a platform truck in the livery of T. Griffin & Son, and seen at the start at Birch. The vehicle is powered by a Gardner 150 diesel engine, and the mascot of a knight can be seen on the radiator.

A 1977 Bedford TK four-wheeled platform truck seen at Birch in 2002. This vehicle was first registered on 4 November 1977. The TK was a popular truck, and there are many restored vehicles on the rally scene. This truck is named 'Emma Jane' after a relative of the owner.

This Leyland Beaver four-wheeled flat truck is seen at Birch. The year of manufacture is uncertain, although it is believed to be pre-1950. It has been seen in a number of liveries between 2010 and the time of compilation. Smartly turned out, it has additional protection fitted on the front bumper.

Roy Dodsworth

A 1979 Leyland Marathon mark two seen at Birch. Manufactured at AEC works, Southall, and introduced in 1977 with a TL12 engine, it was well received. Leyland closed the AEC plant in 1979 and manufacture moved to Scammell at Watford. The TL12 engine was then made at Leyland works. The Leyland Marathon 2 was Truck of the Year in 1981.

This is a 1978 Volvo F86 four-wheeled tipper, its body covered with canvas. This vehicle is always a delight to see. It is in 'working life' condition and I suspect it has had a hard working life. The vehicle is a regular on the local rally scene.

Roy Dodsworth collection 2009

A 1979 Leyland Clydesdale four-wheeled flat truck. Albion also named a truck Clydesdale, and when taken over by British Leyland, the name was carried over. New to an owner in County Durham, then sold and later stored for many years at North Eastern DAF, restoration started in 2001 when only 40,000 miles had been recorded. Seen at Birch, it was entered by Maurice Duckett, who is seen in the cab.

Roy Dodsworth collection 2008

This is a rare vehicle, a 1984 Leyland Landmaster, left-hand drive, built by Leyland Motors Overseas Operations. It was part of a cancelled export order and has been seen at various rallies over the years. The vehicle was in the 9–12-tonne GVW export range and failure was due to general collapse of export markets, particularly in Africa. It was closely related to the T45 Freighter. Seen at Birch and entered by B. Cowgill.

An Atkinson Borderer four-wheeled tractor unit bought new by Bowker in 1974. After road use it was sent to Hull Depot and used as a shunter until 1980. Found semi-derelict in 1993, it has been gradually restored. It is shown coupled to an ex Bowker 1970 Pitt tilt trailer. There are a number of classic commercials restored in the Bowker livery, this one entered by Kevin Battersby.

A 1961 Bristol HA6L tractor unit in the livery of British Road Services, with a sheeted load on the trailer. It operated from BRS Oldbury depot all its working life. Was donated to Walsall Training College, and later disposed of for restoration. The depot code shows IE1045. An imposing vehicle, seen on The Stray.

A 1993 Scania 300 series skip wagon, fitted with an 11-litre diesel engine, seen at Harrogate in the livery of Skippy's Skip Hire. First registered on 1 November 1993, this 300 series is part of a large-model Scania range in the UK. A number of earlier Scania models are seen in preservation.

A 1972 Albion CD21 Clydesdale tipper, fitted with a LAD cab, used by Leyland, Albion and Dodge. It is in the livery of Hoveringham, who were quarry contractors dealing in sand and gravel, sadly no longer in business. First registered in July 1972, it is diesel powered.

A MAN M340 four-axle tractor unit, registered in 1983 and fitted with a 11431 cc diesel engine. Man Truck and Bus are manufactured in Germany and their products are regularly seen in the UK. Over the years the company have produced trucks in partnership with Saviem, a French company, and Volkswagen. In Spain the trucks are badged as Pegaso.

A 1972 Bedford TK four-wheeled tipper, entered by Tony Buckley and in the livery of Ernest Axon. It was used every day until 1999 when it was retired and totally rebuilt in 2000. Unusually, a one-owner vehicle in pristine condition, it is used for promotional purposes. It is seen at Harrogate.

Roy Dodsworth colle

A 1989 Foden 4300 tractor unit in the livery of McMurrays Haulage. New to Kidman Haulage of Huntingdon and manufactured with a Caterpillar engine, which proved troublesome, it was returned to Foden and fitted with a Cummins engine, still in use. Since this picture was taken, it is now in the green and white livery of Chris Henry of Bradford and entered by Phillip Cunnington.

Roy Dodsworth collect

Registered in June 1973, this is a BMC Redline XVE with a Marshall of Cambridge body. Seven other vehicles in the XVE series were also registered by Marshalls on the same day. This one is in the livery of John Lewis Partnership, the other liveries not known. Marshalls would have taken delivery of chassis and cabs and built the bodywork as and when.

A Dodge 500 series four-wheeled flat truck, in the livery of D. J. Donnelly. It is showing registration 8947YZ, and fitted with a Perkins 6354 engine and two-speed axle. This vehicle is badged as a Dodge, but initially this cab style started life as a Commer, and latterly was a Renault.

This is a 1973 Austin FG tipper, with 'threepenny bit' cab. This had a number of advanced features for the safety and comfort of the driver and any passengers. Rear hinged doors gave ease of access, and a good view with the extra cab glazing. Seen in the livery of W. Greenwood & Sons.

A 1989 Atkinson turbo-cooled double-drop-side tipper. It is in the livery of Brianplant and seen at Harrogate. This was manufactured after the Seddon takeover, is Perkins diesel powered, and with the Atkinson Silver Knight mascot on the grille.

New to Shell Mex and BP, this is a 1963 AEC Mercury tractor unit. Now fully restored, it has been fitted with a fifth-wheel ballast box. The first Mercury model appeared in 1928 and the name was resurrected between the 1950s and 1960s. Park Royal designed a cab that was used across the range from 1954. This one is unusual, having a single-piece windscreen. It was entered by G. Tinker.

Roy Dodsworth

This 1956 ERF KV four-wheeled drop-side tipper is in the livery of Gardner, diesel engine makers, and used by them for over 30 years. When Gardner closed, the vehicle went to H. Fleetwood & Sons, delivering parts to the Scottish fishing fleet until 1989. As expected, this vehicle has a Gardner engine, and it was entered by Phillip Cunnington.

Roy Dodsworth collection 2008

This is a 1969 Bedford JC2 light truck. Imported from New Zealand in 2012, it was a prize winner on Trans Pennine in 2014. As well as pickup bodies, the JC2 was built as a box van and a small number of ambulances, some used by West Midlands Ambulance Service. These trucks were imported because generally they were always in good condition due to a good climate, and also because Bedford had stopped making them. Entered by C. Kingdon.

Roy Dodsworth col

A 1966 Austin KF drop-side lorry, it is in original condition and has probably been hard worked. With Morris Commercial, Austin became part of the British Motor Corporation in the 1950s, and as such, identical products could be badged Austin, Morris or BMC.

A 1969 Volvo F88 240 four-wheeled tractor unit, seen in the livery of and entered by Matthew Kibble of Colne, Lancashire. The vehicle has previously been seen towing a 1974 flatbed trailer. The cab style is now rarely seen and was fitted to the larger range of models.

A 1978 ERF series three 'Wrecker' in the livery of West Yorkshire, a National Bus Company, with a head office in Harrogate. Used obviously for bus breakdowns, it is seen at Harrogate. Of interest is the logo of the National Bus Company seen on the door panel. This logo was adopted after nationalisation and was seen on virtually every bus or coach in the UK. Since deregulation the logo became extinct.

AWD took over the manufacture of Bedford trucks when the firm closed down manufacturing at Luton and Dunstable. This four-wheeled recovery truck is quite rare. Bedford's core business of truck making was divested by General Motors to AWD in 1987. When the company collapsed in 1989 it was bought by dealer network Marshall of Cambridge. The production figures were low.

No rally would be the same without a Green Goddess. Based on a Bedford chassis with 4x4 drive, they were intended for civil defence and auxiliary purposes; 2x4 drive versions were also made. Built between 1953 and 1956, they were highly maintained when in government ownership until a decision was made to sell them. This was one of two on The Stray at Harrogate in 2008.

A 1979 ERF M series two-axle flat lorry seen previously in the livery of T. Smith & Sons. The M series was manufactured until early 1990s and sales were generally good, but troubled times were ahead and ERF was taken over by Man Truck and Bus in 2000, who closed the company in 2005.

A 1954 AEC Mercury, in the livery of Roy Cawood, and carrying a meat box converted to living accommodation. This vehicle is unusual in that it has a Bowyer cab, specified separately by the new owner. It is quite common to see preserved trucks with living accommodation. The box van at one time had a mural of the Bisto Kids on the side.

A 1988 DAF 2800 two-axle tractor unit in the livery of V. Pearce, the first owner was Wilsons Transport of Bradford. It has a modular tilting cab and is unusually fitted with three windscreen wipers. Seen at Harrogate, it was entered by Vaughan Pearce.

Roy Dodsworth collection 2009

A 1952 Morris Commercial CV 30 cwt tipper, in the livery of W. Jarvis, and seen at Harrogate. It was registered on 31 March 1952, new to Albion Iron Foundry, and sold by them in 1980 when the firm closed down. It was then mothballed until 1998, with a full restoration finishing in 2004. Morris Commercial CV series were popular with Post Office Telephones, who owned a number of van versions. Entered by Melvyn Blackburn of Middletown.

Roy Dodsworth collection 2009

A 1938 Bedford WL9 furniture removal van, owned by McCarthy's of Leeds. This vehicle was still working when this photograph was taken in 2010, and it was thought to be the oldest working lorry in the UK. In 2012 the vehicle was seen advertised for sale and I have not seen it since.

A 1965 AEC Mammoth Major three-axle tractor unit. It is in the livery of Simon Shelley. This vehicle has the traditional AEC wrap-round windscreen cab and additional bumper protection.

Roy Dods

A fine 1946 Leyland Beaver two-axle drop-side truck. It is in the livery of W. H. Bowker of Blackburn, Lancashire. The firm have a number of classic commercial vehicles and are regular show attenders.

A 1964 Ford Thames Trader two-axle flatbed lorry in the livery of Wareing of Wrea Green, who are suppliers of steel buildings. This is a mark two model, recognised by the position of the words Thames and Trader.

Roy D

A 1970 Atkinson two-axle tractor unit, towing a high-sided tipping trailer, again with two axles, seen in the livery of R. W. Morris. Powered by a Gardner diesel engine, it has additional front bumper protection.

A 1966 International two-axle tractor unit coupled to a box trailer. Seen in the livery of Bradley of Accrington, who have a number of classic commercials regularly shown at local events. Another example of a truck made at Doncaster by International Harvester, it has a traditional grey grille and a butterfly bonnet.

Roy Dodsworth collection 2009

This is a 1971 Scammell Routeman tractor unit with three axles: the front two single wheeled and the third double wheeled. The vehicle is coupled to a 30,000-litre tanker and was new to Shell Mex and BP, in whose livery it was. The current owner has removed the Shell and BP markings and it is now in plain black. When in service the vehicles covered high mileage across the UK.

Registered in 1985, Ford Trans Continental 4428, in the livery of Bailey's Transport, it was new to Sea-Mar Heavy Haulage. Probably one of the last made, as production ceased in 1984. There were 8735 made, 8231 in Amsterdam and 504 at Foden works in Sandbach, Cheshire. Cab supplied by Berliet, fitted with a Cummins engine. Noted for having an oil and water meter in the cab.

Roy Dodsworth collection 2009

A 1948 Foden 094/6 two-axle flat truck, fitted with a Gardner diesel engine. In the livery of G. & H. Donaldson & Sons. On the truck is living accommodation, commonly seen at rallies and usually fitted out with rest and cooking facilities.

Roy Dodsworth collection 2009

A 1951 Bedford OSBT two-axle recovery truck, in the livery of and entered by C. J. Elsworth of Barnoldswick, it is seen at Harrogate. This model was very popular and Bedford also made models as trucks and buses in the OB range. The Bedford OB was a successful single decker and coach.

Roy Dodsworth collection 2009

Roy Dodsw[...]

A 1961 Foden S21 two-axle tipper, it started life as a concrete mixer, fitted with a five-cylinder Gardner engine and a four-speed gearbox, now changed to a Foden 12-speed. The tipper body has been fitted with 'greedy boards', which allow extra load. In the livery of Sam Long, of Chapel-en-le-Frith and entered by D. Pickup.

A 1948 Leyland Comet two-axle lorry. Seen with a covered load in the livery of P. M. Clayton, Bradford. The vehicle has been previously seen as a fairground lorry in 1982, carrying equipment for 'Span the Week', a fairground attraction.

Roy Dodsworth collection 2009

A 1966 Scammell Highwayman ballast tractor, two axles and fitted with a Gardner 150 diesel engine. Although the current owner is not known, it has been seen in the livery of Swansea Truck Centre. Seen here at Harrogate, the Highwayman was a popular tractor unit for general haulage, and with fuel suppliers.

Roy Dodsworth collection 2009

A 1955 Atkinson L1856 four-axle flat truck in the livery of Hague Transport of Ormskirk, Lancashire. This model is a rarity, as few four-axle vehicles were made, and are also rare in preservation.

A 1966 Albion Claymore FT25N in the livery of Eastern Plant Service. It is fitted with an underfloor engine and has a spacious cab. Identical vehicles badged as Leyland exist. The vehicle and dog have been seen at a number of previous rallies.

Roy Dodsworth collection 2009

A 1984 Scammell three-axle Crusader ballast tractor. New to Rochdale Electric Welding for heavy haulage, it had STGO CAT 2 certification for use in moving heavy or abnormal loads. This was a popular-selling vehicle for Scammell. Seen at Harrogate, it was entered by J. Ingoe.

Roy Dodsworth collection 2009

A 1962 ERF KV box van, PEN897, in the livery of Bensons Sweets of Bury. This was on the ERF show stand at the 1962 Commercial Motor Show at Earls Court. A number of other Benson vans were also registered PEN. Later sold to Henry Long Transport at Bradford, it was used by them for a short time and was then reliveried into a subsidiary, George Pickersgill Removals. It was subsequently disposed of and rebuilt back into Bensons livery. Following the death of the owner, an advert in a truck magazine appeared offering the truck for sale: '1962 £16500. Well known on the show scene, starts on the button, 4 beds, cooker, sink, fridge etc.' Hopefully when sold we may see it out and about again. Entered, when photographed, by the late George Wassell.

Roy Dodsworth collection 2009

A 1994 Seddon Atkinson Strato 1741C Knight of the Road. Seen in fine condition in the livery of Taylor's Transport of Oldham, at Harrogate. Owners of large trucks like to fit additional lighting and bumper bars, which gives a macho appearance. Trucks of today and those over 20 years old are the classic trucks of tomorrow.

Roy Dodsworth collection 20

A brightly coloured 1958 Mack B61 Thermidore three-axle tractor unit, made in Maryland, Ohio, USA. The B models were a primary vehicle for manufacture, and since 1953 some 127,786 models were made. Mack trucks are still in production. 'King of the Road' on the bumper is a macho indication of the power and size of the vehicle.

KING OF THE ROAD

976 XUH

A 1961 AEC Mammoth Major four-axle 'Wrecker' fitted with a 9.6-litre diesel engine. The owner's premises are in Huddersfield, adjacent to the M62, and it is used for towing and recovery of vehicles.

A Dennis 30 cwt van, built in 1931. Vehicles of this type were popular because they attracted a lower tax-bracket payment: there was a payment of £50 per year for three years, on condition that the vehicle was in good condition for call-up, if necessary, for war purposes. Has had two restorations, first by Jack Sparshatt, then a second by the current owners, Howarth Brothers Transport, Royton, Lancashire, who used their livery when completed.

A 1976 Volvo F86 two-axle tractor unit in the livery of Howarth Brothers of Royton. Seen carrying a vintage truck, a Model T, at Harrogate.

Roy Dodsworth collection 2009

A 1950 Foden 094/6 two-axle tipper seen in the livery of British Road Services, North Nottinghamshire, with depot code 63E248. Won the 'Mayor's Choice' when judging took place at Harrogate in 2009.

Roy Dodsworth collection 2009

A 1962 Austin FHK two-axle drop-side truck with a payload of eight tons, forward control and with a chrome grille surround. In the livery of Jess Turner, Potato Merchant.

Roy Dodsworth collection 2009

A 1926 Ford Model TT1 pickup in the livery of L. W. B. motors. The vehicle was manufactured at the Ford Plant, Trafford Park, Manchester, and is fitted with bun-type oil lamps. The vehicle was bought at auction in 2014 for £7500. Seen on a low loader at Birch for eventual unloading and display at Harrogate.

A 1951 ERF LK44. New to Ernest Bradshaw, Millers and Corn Merchants of Driffield, East Yorkshire, now seen in the livery of A. Sharratt of Worsley, Manchester. The owner and his wife seem content with the weather and the ambience of their surroundings.

Tel: WOR 7507

ERF

~Rachel~

H 23

KWF 850

A 1980 Leyland Marathon two-axle tractor unit, owned by John Tweedie of Skipton, who has converted the Leyland into a badged AEC. The Marathon did not feature in their model range. John supports a number of local rallies during the summer months and owns a Bedford TK lorry.

Roy Dodsworth collection 2009

Collecting old military vehicles is very popular and many specialised events are organised. This is a 1941 Bedford O-type cargo used in WW2, fitted with a canvas tilt. Military vehicles make excellent diecast models and the O type is popular in the BT model range.

A 1971 Foden S39 three-axle tractor in the livery of A. Appleyard of Wakefield. This is designed for the heavy jobs. S39 models were big sellers until a model change in 1979. It has the traditional model range GRP cab.

Roy Dodsworth collection 2009

A 1974 Atkinson Borderer two-axle tractor unit, fitted with a Cummins diesel engine, it is in the livery of L. J. Brumpton & Son. It has an additional hazard warning at the front bumper. An identical Atkinson is alongside.

A 1969 BMC FG drop-side tipper. Fitted with a 'threepenny bit' cab, it is in the livery of R. Tinker, welding engineers of Manchester. When introduced, the cab was considered revolutionary. The doors were rear hinged and opened out towards the body, giving easy access to the cab, and additional windows gave increased vision to the road ahead. Tinkers have a number of classic commercials with which they support the Trans Pennine.

This is a 1945 three-axle Leyland Hippo in the livery of Davis Brothers, London and Warrington. Seen with a traditional roped and sheeted load, rarely seen today, it was built just after the end of WW2 and it is regularly seen out on the rally field. This type of Leyland was also used by the Forces during WW2.

Roy Dodsworth collection

Seen at Harrogate, this is a 1949 two-axle Foden S18 flat lorry. Fitted with a diesel engine, it is in the livery of J. & M. Macfarlane of Kirby Lonsdale, in the former county of Westmorland, now Cumbria. The S18 cab was also used on the FG range and adopted the same type of front grille panel.

This is a 1930 Dennis drop-side truck in the livery of Howarth Bros Haulage of Oldham. Vehicles of this type were extremely popular as they attracted a lower tax rate. This was because the government planned to have a supply of suitable vehicles available for use in the event of further conflict. Howarth's have a collection of classic vehicles and are keen supporters of the event.

A 1964 Foden S21A four-axle bulk carrier in the livery of Horace Kendrick of Walsall, Staffs. It has a cab nicknamed 'Mickey Mouse', a name used by the press; prior to this, Sputnik and Spaceship were often used. The vehicle has been painted by renowned vehicle artist Mike Jeffries, and a greetings card featuring the vehicle was available on Amazon in the past.

Roy Dodsworth collection 2010

A 1958 Bedford A3 fire engine fitted with a 3200CC petrol engine. The cab is also familiar as a Chevrolet. The fire-tender bodywork is somewhat primitive and it is presumed it was used as a works fire engine. It now has 'Governors Bay Volunteer Fire Brigade' on the side, indicating that this is one of many Bedfords of this type imported from New Zealand.

Roy Dodsw

A 1989 ERF E10 new to TDG Distribution, now in the livery of F. Smith Bulk Carriers. The two-axle tractor unit is coupled to a bulk sheeted tipping trailer. Note the registration unique to the vehicle. Alongside is a later ERF variant.

Roy Dodsworth collection 2009

Roy Dodsworth collection 2009

A 1976 Leyland Buffalo two-axle tractor unit coupled to a curtain-sider trailer. Curtain-sider, as the name implies, means that the side sheets can be opened to make unloading easier with a forklift truck or similar. Entered by A. Brierley, a regular supporter of the event with his fleet of preserved vehicles.

DOUBLE DIAMOND

IND COOPE & ALLSOPP

R. TINKER
BUILDING ENGINEERS

MDE·804

This is a 1950 Morris Commercial FV flat truck used as a brewer's dray. Purchased by the present owner in 2001, a rebuild took over three years to complete. Seen in Ind Coope & Allsopp Burton livery, who were brewers of Double Diamond and stout.

A 1949 Leyland Octopus, new to BRS Camberwell in 1950. Worked at various London depots before transfer to Sheffield, depot code 53A773, when it was sold to a Lancashire showman then bought for preservation in 1981. BRS had a large fleet of these vehicles.

A 1983 Bedford TL two-axle rigid flat, fitted with a horse transporter box, in the livery of P. R. Croft. The horsebox can easily be removed, allowing general use of the truck.

A 1953 AEC Militant three-axle cargo truck, seen with a canvas tilt. AEC built a large number of military vehicles for use during WW2. A model of this type of vehicle was made by Dinky Toys as a Supertoy.

A 1980 ERF B series recovery vehicle. Fitted with a 12-litre diesel engine, it is in the livery of DAS transport of Cottingham, Hull, East Yorkshire, and entered by D. Shores. In 1972 Jack Cooke, a former Atkinson engineer, joined ERF and took part in the development of a new groundbreaking cab. The subsequent steel-framed fibreglass-panelled steel/plastic cab was fitted to the B series.

Roy Dodsworth collection 2

A 1953 Albion Chieftain FT 37 two-axle flat truck, which was new to Bennetts of Ossett and later restored by Colin Pitt. Acquired by its present owner in 2006, it is now in the livery of Tuer's Motors, a company that was established over 80 years ago and who operated a number of Albion vehicles.

A 1976 Seddon Atkinson 400 series articulated unit, in the livery of National Carriers Bradford. The company was a later part of the National Freight Corporation set up by the Thatcher government. A frequent attender at local events.

A mystery vehicle, at first possibly similar to a Leyland Landmaster seen earlier in the book. This is registered as a Volvo, having a Volvo chassis and engine. The keen enthusiast will identify that the cab is the top half of a Bedford TK, making a unique cab design. Fitted out as a 'wrecker', it is diesel powered. It is known as a 'bitsa' – bits of this and bits of that! Entered by Paul Sweeting.

A 1960 Morris FF two-axle rigid fitted with a four-litre diesel engine, and a drop-side body covered with a canvas, it is in the livery of John Andrew & Son. Vehicle new to a coal merchant in Cheadle, Staffordshire and used until 1988.

This 1967 forward control Bedford is a ten-tonne gross threeway tipper. It was imported from New Zealand and restored in UK. It has a three-litre engine running on petrol or LPG. The 'threeway' of the name indicates that the body has a conventional tip and also cab tip left or right, useful for road repairs with tarmac. Vehicles were imported, with little or no rust, due to climate, and because production in the UK had stopped.

Roy Dodsworth collection 2(

A 1974 Atkinson Borderer, fitted with a Cummins diesel, an articulated unit in the livery of Comfortex, foam converters of Rochdale, and occasionally used for business. Owned by Ray Beckwith, it is seen at many events through the year. Prior to Comfortex ownership it was seen in livery of Marson and Darlow and used as a recovery vehicle.

Roy D ion 20

Seen here is a 1936 Bedford WLG two-tonner flat truck with a tailboard, owned and driven by Steve Hullah, in whose livery it is shown. Designated as fleet number 2, it has on display two AA badges (the silver one is pre-war) and a Bedford Drivers Club (BDC) badge. A brass fire extinguisher, possibly of Angus manufacture, is shown fitted to the headboard.

A 1947 Albion A25N petrol engine flat truck, in the livery of R. Tinker Ltd. It was new to Campbell's Motor Services, Aberdeen, and rescued from a scrapyard in 1975. The company support Trans Pennine regularly with their fleet of classic commercials. Seen on the open space of The Stray, due to early arrival from Birch Services.

A 1954 Morris FVS two-axle rigid. Morris only made this model for 18 months, producing only 849, and this is thought to be the only one remaining. Seen with a sheeted load, it was found derelict and was restored by John Andrew & Sons. A sister vehicle from the fleet was parked alongside. This is a very welcome long-distance entry from Launceston in Cornwall.

Roy Dodsworth collection 2009

Probably the most popular vehicle on The Stray, a Scania R480 articulated unit operated by Huntapac. This is a company owned by the Hunter family, who since the 1990s generously have provided two packed lunches per driver entrant. Several vehicles from the Hunter Collection also enter the event. Thank you!

Roy Dodsworth collection 2009

Roy Dodsworth collection 2009

A 1978 lightweight Ford D series two-axle rigid. The sheeted load covers living accommodation. The D series was a successor to the Thames Trader. In the livery of Roy Lockwood of Barnsley.

A Volvo fire and rescue vehicle from the North Yorkshire Fire Authority. Running an event such as Trans Pennine requires co-operation from the police, fire and ambulance services and St John's First Aid volunteers. Two firefighters are seen with the vehicle. Their presence is greatly appreciated.

A 1959 Ford Thames Trader two-axle drop-side. It was purchased in a farm sale in 2007 with only 24,500 recorded miles by the previous owner, then taken off the road in early 1970s and kept in farm buildings. Now restored and painted in original livery, its entry to the 2009 event was the first time out, driven by William Banks.

A 1959 AEC Mercury four-axle rigid in the livery of and entered by Richard Cresswell & Sons of Hilderstone. The platform body was built by Cravens Homalloy, usually carrying one of a number of vintage tractors. Seen at Harrogate and entered by Phillip Cunnington, it spent all its working life in Lincolnshire hauling potatoes.

A 1975 Atkinson Borderer tractor unit, restored in the livery of Hoyer Bulk Liquid Transport of Huddersfield. To conform to the Carrying of Dangerous Substances Regulations, the exhaust pipe has had to be removed from the back of the vehicle to the front as a precaution in the event of fire.

This is a 1976 Scammell Crusader two-axle recovery vehicle owned by Richardson's Garage, Wellydale Road, Oldham, Greater Manchester. The vehicle is named 'Wellydale Crusader'.

Roy Dodsworth collection 2009

Roy Dodsworth collection 2009

A 1948 AEC Mammoth Major eight-axle flat truck. New to Express Dairies in Devon, then on general haulage in Wales, until found by its present owner in a Dundee scrapyard. Restored in 2004, it is a fine example of early post-war transport. Miles Fox has other classic commercials and they are seen at local events during the summer.

A Leyland Comet 90, which was new to Lancashire County Council. It is fitted with tar-spreading equipment and was used on road construction. Taken out of service in 1972, it was later sold on for use on the Isle of Arran. With its present owner since 1993, it has been restored as a replica in the livery of the London Brick Company.

Roy Dodsworth collection 2009

A 1969 two-axle Foden S36 tractor unit. In the livery of Slaters Transport and under contract to Tilcon, whose name appears in the livery. Tilcon use a lot of owner-drivers, who use and maintain their own vehicles.

Roy Dodsworth collection 2009

A 1956 Guy Otter diesel engine two-axle rigid, which was new to Wednesbury Tube Company and since restored. It is fitted with a Boalloy cab with a wrap-round windscreen. Boalloy cabs were specified on a number of different trucks as an option to factory fitted.

Roy Dodsworth collection 2009

Roy Dodsw

A 1956 Atkinson Silver Knight two-axle tractor unit. It is in the livery of M. S. Chapman and has a front bumper attachment with a towing hook and additional lighting.

A 1952 three-axle Foden S20, originally built as a cement mixer. It was sold into fairground work and fitted with a fifth wheel. With its present owner since 2001, it has had a major rebuild, including a coach-built cab. In the livery of heavy-haulage specialists Elliott of York.

Roy Dodsworth collection

A 1950 Leyland Beaver two-axle rigid, possibly unrestored, seen at Harrogate. The load could be living accommodation, which is proving popular with frequent rally attenders. It has been seen with a cattle-carrying box previously. A Huntapac lunch bag awaits attention!

A 1961 Foden FG6/15 S20 three-axle rigid, new to Aluminium Corporation of Dolgarrog, North Wales, it is fitted with a Gardner 6LW engine, a two-'stick' 12-speed gearbox with a single-drive axle. Owned and driven by Malcolm Bright, who also owns and drives a restored Foden single-decker bus.

A 1942 GMC CCKW 353 truck. From Barnoldswick, Lancashire, it saw active service in WW2 and is a frequent attender on the Trans Pennine. Entered by W. T. Gissing, this vehicle has been a prize winner for best truck driven by a lady, Mrs Ann Gissing. The Yorkshire Military Vehicle Trust kindly arranges a display for the event.

A 1969 Leyland Super Comet, ERGO-cabbed, two-axle rigid. Part of the Hunter Collection, it is in the livery of H. Hunter, Hay and Straw Merchant. ERGO is short for ergonomics, which means the applied science of design and arranging things so that people can use things that interact efficiently and safely!

A 1952 AEC Mammoth Major three-axle rigid with a flat body. New to the RAF as a refuelling tanker, it then worked at the Royal Ordnance factory, Euxton. It is now restored in its present state in the fleet of Jess Turner.

A 1959 AEC Mercury tractor unit seen at Harrogate. New to H. Dando of Chipping Sodbury, later passing to Neil James. Found in rough condition in 2005 and since restored.

A 1959 AEC Mammoth Major, six-wheeled rigid flat truck, in the livery of A. & H. Hardy. The sheeted load disguises living accommodation, and the fixture on top of the cab provided storage for unused sheeting, which was a theft deterrent.

A fine vehicle with history, this is a 1936 Albion 5505PL. New to Barrett's of Wood Green, London, it later passed to Henry Thurston, a showman, and was used as a dodgem carrier. Acquired by the present owners in 1978 and restored by them in their livery of E. M. Rogers of Northampton.

Roy Dodsworth collection 2009

A 1954 Guy Otter two-axle rigid, fitted with a Gardner diesel, it has a drop-side body which is sheeted, and in the livery of and entered by Len Isherwood of Bacup. Spent its first year with Middleton Tyres, then seven years with two farmers before restoration. It is a regular attender at Trans Pennine.

Roy Dodsworth collection 20

A 1938 Albion LB40 two-axle rigid, fitted with a petrol engine, it has a flat platform body which is carrying an authentic textile load. In the livery of C. & C. Textiles, who are regular attenders at local events.

Roy Dodsworth collection

A 1939 Scammell 6x4 Rigid 6 (R6) fitted with a drop-side body, new to the Post Office Stores Department, Birmingham. When sold off, it was seen as a flat truck in plain colours, used by a London firm hauling surplus army clothes. Then it was operated by Hallett Silberman for Mallet Porter & Sons, subsequently being rescued from a breaker's yard then slowly restored back to the original specification. Some time later it was damaged by fire and had a second restoration as seen today.

Roy Dodsworth co

Roy Dodsworth collection 2009

A 1980 ERF LV, two axles, fitted with a livestock-carrying body. In the livery of A. Janes & Sons, it has unusual but very effective varnish paintwork. It has been seen on previous rallies towing a livestock-carrying container.

Roy Dodsworth collection 20

A 1944 ERF C1 two-axle rigid with a flat platform body and carrying a vintage Ferguson tractor. It is in the livery of J. Scott & Sons and is seen on a low-loader at Birch prior to setting off for Harrogate.

A 1933 Morris Commercial C-type flat truck. Used on the road until 1946, it spent the rest of its life working on a farm. Restored in 1976, it has appeared in a number of film and television adverts. It is parked here at Birch, awaiting a start for Harrogate, entered by A. Kayley.

A 1959 AEC two-axle rigid with a Homalloy cab and a box body. A. Brierley are keen supporters of Trans Pennine and two of their other vehicles feature in this book.

A 1942 AEC Matador 4x4 recovery truck, a vehicle with lots of history. New to the British Army, it left service in 1947 and was then bought by Bradford Corporation, used for towing/recovery of trolley buses and motor buses. Allocated fleet number 081, it was garaged at Ludlam Street and used trade plates 065AK or 164KU. In January 1970 it was registered for the first time and it had a complete overhaul and rebuild at Thornbury works. The engine, gearbox and other mechanical parts were upgraded from the multiple spares available at the garage. In 1974, along with all other Bradford Corporation transport vehicles, it became part of West Yorkshire Metro bus company.

A 1956 Bedford S-type two-axle rigid fitted with sheeted drop-side body. New to Auxiliary Fire Service, it is in the livery of T. Brierley and is a regular entry on local rallies.

A 1988 Volvo FLT eight-wheeled 'logger' with fitted stakes and a lorry-mounted crane. An ideal vehicle for transporting heavy loads of wood to the sawmills. Seen at Harrogate.

This is a 1976 Volvo F88 articulated unit used for transporting a Bedford fire tender to Birch, where it is unloaded and then driven along with the Volvo to Harrogate.

The official War Office designation for this vehicle is 'Truck. three ton. 4x4 Fire tender – (Bedford QL)'. During its military service (in WW2) it was fitted with a special body, a water tank with 200-gallon capacity, and a PTO-driven pump along with tilt framework and cover; it also towed a trailer pump. When released from military service, it was allocated to Lancashire County Fire Service and served at Morecambe Bay. Seen locally at rallies in the season, and entered by Michael Joy.

A Dodge Commando two-axle rigid with a beavertail body. Whilst registered in 1986, it was first owned by British Airways and worked on the runway at Heathrow, unregistered, for four years, with a scissor lift catering hoist body supplying food and beverages for various airlines. Now in the livery of Lannens Turf Supplies, Bradford, who own the vehicle.

A 1965 Leyland Octopus four-axle tanker in the livery of Bristol Omnibus Company, part of the National Bus Corporation. New to Shell Mex and BP, it was restored and entered by John Murphy. A stunning-looking vehicle. Leyland Octopuses were popular with tanker operators.

This is a 1966 Albion tractor unit, fitted with a LAD cab used by Leyland, Albion and Dodge. It is coupled to a low-loader trailer, single axle and twin wheels. Owned and used by E. Bailey & Sons of Mottram, Greater Manchester. The company also own a restored Bedford TK and another Albion. Always immaculately turned out, it is pictured at the halfway stop, Harry Ramsden's fish and chip shop, Guiseley.

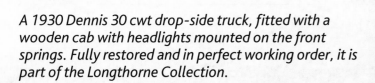

A 1930 Dennis 30 cwt drop-side truck, fitted with a wooden cab with headlights mounted on the front springs. Fully restored and in perfect working order, it is part of the Longthorne Collection.

A 1927 Leyland FE1. A rare vehicle with no cab, open-air driving. Note the wooden wheels and solid tyres. Large brass headlights are fitted, with additional lighting at the top of the dashboard area.

Vehicles of this era have starting handles, as this is the only way to start the vehicle. Strong muscles are needed. Part of the Longthorne Collection.

A 1956 Dennis Pax in the livery of brewers Whitbread and depicting a typical brewer's dray. It is powered by a Perkins diesel engine, and previously was in the livery of A. T. Lough Haulage. Entered by Geoff Walker.

A 1940 Bedford MW recovery truck. Vehicle new to the Army for use during WW2, the cab is the general style of the Bedford range throughout this period. It was converted to a recovery truck in 2005. Entered by Bob Parker of Penrith.

Roy Dodsworth collection 2015

Roy Dodsworth collection 2015

A 1940 Bedford MW recovery truck. New to the Army, it saw service during the war, and is seen with a semitrailer, which has a Scammell coupling. It is powered by a Perkins diesel and was entered by Bob Parker of Penrith, who also owns the vehicle in the previous photo.

A 1962 AEC Mercury tractor unit and trailer in the livery of Heeley Bros Ltd, and bearing 2 RHA (Road Haulage Association) stickers. The cab, maker unknown, is not standard AEC fitting.

Here is a 1966 Austin FG flat truck, a BMC (British Motor Corporation) product also seen badged as BMC or Morris. Fitted with a BMC diesel as indicated on the badge plate, displayed together with a BMC Drivers Club badge. Also shown on front of cab are the names Karen, Winnie and Georgia. It is in the smart livery of H. Kershaw & Sons, Oldham, and seen loaded with empty textile skips.

A 1956 Leyland Octopus four-axle flat truck. Entered by the Hunter Collection, founded by the late William Hunter. Octopus vehicles were a favourite of Mr Hunter, and in the collection is another one, red coloured and liveried in his name. This one is in the livery of Walter Southworth, of Rufforth, Lancashire, who were on contract to Guinness to transport vats of draught Guinness.

A 1996 Volvo FL10 intercooler tractor unit and trailer entering Birch Services M62. The vehicle is carrying a 'tired' Foden half-cab dumper. Entered by J. Pickersgill.

Roy Dodsworth collection 2015

This is 'Big Mal', a 4x4 dump truck introduced in 1954. A version with a four-cylinder Foden engine was shown at the Commercial Vehicle Show that year. Also entered by J. Pickersgill.

A 1974 Atkinson Defender four-axle unit fitted with a cattle-remover body, it is fitted with a Cummins diesel. This is a remarkable restoration, the woodworking on the body and loading platform showing joinery skills used to a good effect. Entered by J. Brownbridge.

An AEC Mammoth Major Mk111-6, with a flat body, in the livery of James C. Ashworth, a Bradford haulier, sadly long gone. Seen with extra carrying space over the cab, it was most likely used to carry bales of wool – two extra bales would be above the cab. Ashworth's were also well known for transporting International Tractors, from the Idle works to Doncaster. Entered by M. Gill.

A 1918 ex-War Department Daimler. First registration details not known, but it was re-registered DM3161 in 1928. Fitted with a flat body, it was found in Wales with the remains of a bus or charabanc body. It was seen in a 2012 auction catalogue with a sale estimate of £18,000/£24,000. Owned by Ken Longthorne, it arrived on a low-loader at Harrogate.

On the same low-loader as the previous vehicle, was this Leyland PH five-tonner. New as KE9677 to Maidstone & District as a single-deck bus, it was re-registered in 1928 as UV6025 with a flat platform body as seen. Ken Longthorne, the owner, told me that some person attempted to steal the brass lamps from the vehicle at an event in 2014.

A Seddon Mark 5S built in 1961, although it was not registered until 1990. In the intervening 29 years it operated, unregistered, in the grounds of an aircraft factory. In previous years it has appeared on the rally field in the livery of Colin Pitt of Otley, and is now owned by Frank Petch, a team member organising the annual events.

A 1954 Atkinson L745L two-axle rigid with a flat body. Used by its first owner on general haulage for ten years, then sold into fairground use, it is now owned by John Clarke. It was restored over the last 18 months, and has additional front bumper attachment.

A 1964 Bedford TJ truck with a well-joinered drop-side body. This model was a popular workhorse and seen in many guises, including ambulances. Entered by Joe Bennett.

Roy Dodswo

A 1953 Thornycroft Trusty PFQR6, which was new to BRS Stratford Group, London, fleet number 66A343. Later transferred to Southampton district in 1956, in 1962 it was sold by auction to Rushgreen Motors. It was bought for preservation in 1988 by Leonard Nield, and there followed an extensive restoration.

This is the crest of British Road Services as seen on the previous vehicle, used on all red and green coloured BRS vehicles and also on Pickford's vehicles. It can be seen on a number of BRS vehicles featured in the book. Pre transfer, digital printing, vinyl coverings and the like, such crests were hand painted by skilled craftsmen.

A 1960 Leyland Octopus eight-axle with a flat platform body, seen in the livery of William Hunter, and part of the Hunter Collection. Shown entering the showground at Harrogate followed by a Leyland Badger, also from the collection. This was the favourite vehicle of the late William Hunter, who died in 2014.

Roy Dods'

This is a Leyland Badger tractor unit, of which the restoration was finished in 2016. It is in the base colour in which these vehicles were delivered. It is coupled to a four-in-line platform trailer in Irish Roadways livery, and is from the Hunter Collection.

Seen here is a 1979 Kenworth W900A, a Class 8 truck in USA. W stands for Worthington, and it is still in production after 50 years. With many options, this is powered by a Cummins engine, but Paccar power was also available; 18-, 13- or 10-speed gearboxes were also available. It is christened 'Sweet Thing'!

A 1970 Atkinson Gold Knight eight-axle tipper, formerly owned by R. Hanson & Son, it is now privately owned and restored. This vehicle has the 20,000th chassis made by Atkinson. R. Hanson operated a large number of eight-wheelers, all in a distinctive livery. It is entered by L. Buxton.

Roy Dodsworth collection 2015

Roy Do

A 1964 Foden S20 eight-wheeler bulk grain carrier. It is powered by a Foden two-stroke engine and fitted with a Mickey Mouse cab. Rescued from Skelton's scrapyard, Peterborough, as a chassis only, it is now fully restored and in the livery of Kenneth Wilson of Leeds. Their livery changed to blue and yellow in the 1960s.

Roy Dodsworth collection 2

RICHARDSONS

RICHARDSONS
OLDHAM

WMP 63

Roy D

A 1951 Atkinson L1586 four-axle rigid fitted with a flat body. New to Nestlé's Chocolate as a tanker and sold by them to a showman and fitted with a van body. It was bought for preservation in 1981 and rebuilt as a platform lorry, and is now in the livery of Richardsons of Oldham, who entered the vehicle. Note the starter handle secured by rubber to the lamp mounting.

A 1951 Vulcan two-axle rigid with a flat sheeted load.
Its first owner was a southern potato haulier and it was
later found in a derelict condition in Northallerton.
Fitted with a Perkins diesel, it was restored in the livery
of Colin Pitt about 20 years ago.

Roy Dodsworth collection 2015

Roy Dodsw

A 1960 Mack B61 tractor unit, left-hand drive, made in
Ohio, USA. In the livery of Braithwaite's Excavations.
One of 127,786 B models made, and entered by Robert
Braithwaite.

A 1959 Saurer Berna 2DM. Made at the Saurer factory in Arbon, Switzerland. New to the Swiss army, it is right-hand drive and has a general cargo body. Usually vehicles made in Switzerland are left-hand drive. Bought from a dealer in Germany and entered by R. Newell.

Roy Dodsworth collection 2015

A 1919 Albion A10 drop-side truck in the livery of Pratts Spirit. Owned and restored by Andy Gibb, the vehicle won Concours d'Elégance at the 2013 HCVS Brighton Run. Andy has restored a number of Albion vehicles over the years, including the Lyons' Cocoa Albion seen earlier in the book. Pictured in the grounds of Harrogate College in 2012, following heavy rain and a flooded Stray.

Another action shot of a tender carrying two vehicle entries to the start at Birch Services. The front vehicle is a Scammell Highwayman ballast tractor, and the second vehicle is a Thornycroft Nubian, ex RAF, now a recovery vehicle.

This is a Thornycroft Nubian built for the RAF. It is now equipped as a recovery vehicle with a five-ton capacity crane and a five-ton winch, and powered by an eight-cylinder Rolls-Royce petrol engine. In the livery of Shire Aggregates of Boroughbridge, it is seen entering the Harrogate College grounds.

This is a 1951 Bedford OSS chassis and cab, under restoration, seen entering Harrogate College grounds in 2012. In 2013 I saw it at another event, with a smart, varnished drop-side timber body.

DBV 487

In 2012 The Stray at Harrogate was flooded. This caused a major problem, solved by the courtesy of the Principal at Harrogate College who allowed the use of the college grounds. As can be seen, it was a tight fit to get vehicles displayed.

Roy Dodsworth collection 2012

This is a Studebaker Reo M35, formerly USA military. It is a 6x4 general cargo vehicle, left-hand drive, and is a regular attender at local rallies.

A 1968 Chevrolet recovery truck made in the USA, left-hand drive. This was originally used as an aircraft tug. Entered by Jonathan Hoyes.

A 1958 Hanomag L28 cargo truck with a covered body. Seen entering The Stray in dry dusty conditions. Made in Germany and left-hand drive.

Roy Dodsworth collection 20

A 1933 Leyland Beaver in the livery of W. H. Bowker of Blackburn. This vehicle was seen in the 1980s as a regular in the HCVS Brighton rally. At that time the spare wheel was mounted on the offside door of the cab. Vehicles in the Bowker livery are regularly seen on local rallies.

This is a 1969 Mack RS-700L three-axle ballast tractor in the livery of Mammoet, entered by G. Mallinson. It was made in Ohio, USA, and is left-hand drive, and seen arriving at Harrogate. Mammoet are specialist engineers in moving large loads.

OVERSIZE

MCW 154G

THE
CEMENT MARKETING COMPANY
LTD.

FERROCRETE

NUW 252

NUW 252

Roy

An early Leyland Comet, restored in the livery of the Cement Marketing Company, 'Ferrocrete', and part of the Hunter Collection. Seen making a dusty entry to The Stray. Dinky Toys made a Supertoy of a like vehicle fitted with grey rubber tyres.

A 1939 Bedford OXD General Service truck fitted with a canvas tilt. It bears Army fleet number L182507 and is fitted with a 3.5-litre straight-six petrol engine. It was first registered on 1 August 1974, when disposed of by the Army authorities. Is owned and driven by R. Cheetham.

Roy Dodsworth co

A 1967 AEC Mandator 294RA four-wheel rigid, fitted with a flat platform body, and seen in the livery of P. J. Curling of Worcestershire. This vehicle was built in 1962 for part of an export order, but partway through the takeover by British Leyland the order was cancelled. It then stood unfinished at the Southall works for four years, due to the introduction of a newer, faster and more comfortable ERGO-cabbed model. It was acquired by Lex Tillotson, a garage group in London, then sold on to an unknown haulier in 1967, when it was first registered. It was then used for two years until parked up and finally restored as seen. Entered by G. Mellor.

A 1980 ERF M series two-axle rigid with a curtain-sider body. In the livery of L. & K. R. Thorpe. It is still a working vehicle, delivering in Teesside three days a week. Entered by Keith Thorpe.

Here is a 1977 Bedford TK recovery vehicle in the livery of Coates Garage. Seen entering The Stray at Harrogate. Since this picture was taken, the vehicle has changed hands and is now in the livery of Yorkshire Rider, fleet number 9502.

A 1959 Leyland Beaver tractor unit with box trailer in the livery of Tesco. This was brought by trailer to Harrogate for its first public display after restoration by the Hunter Collection. New to Smiths of Eccles as fleet number 165.

A 1953 Leyland Comet two-axle tractor unit, fitted with a 2395 cc diesel engine. It is in the livery of J. A. Ford and seen coupled to a single-axle, double-wheeled trailer with a partially sheeted load. The Comet first appeared in 1947 and lasted until 1956 when the series two was announced.

A powerful-looking 1963 Foden S21 tanker in the livery of Tate & Lyle, sugar refiners. It has a Mickey Mouse cab, also known as Sputnik or Satellite. The load of granulated sugar is discharged by means of a blower. The Tate & Lyle livery on the tanker was created by the London-based DRU (Design Research Unit), who also designed the BR logo and also signage for Watneys Brewery.

A 1980 Scammell Routeman four-axle tanker with diesel engine, and in the livery of Blue Circle Cement. The cab was designed by Giovanni Michelotti, a renowned designer who penned the Triumph Herald, Leyland National Bus and numerous Ferraris! The tank carried bulk dry cement, which when on site was air pumped into silos, prior to becoming ready-mixed concrete.

A 1987 Dennis 12-ton flatbed brewer's dray, fitted with a 6502 cc diesel engine, seen in the livery of Whitbread, who were big users of Dennis vehicles. Drays were always fitted with chains to secure barrels when in transit. Wooden barrels are now making a return, due to the popularity of craft ales.

A 1943 ERF C1 FR two-wheel drop-side truck in the striking livery of R. Somerset. Manufactured just prior to the end of WW2, they were popular with haulage contractors. It was first registered 19 October 1943 and is diesel powered.

A 1954 Leyland Comet series one two-axle drop-side truck, seen in the livery of Stanley Skinner, Millers. The tarpaulin hides a load, which is in fact living accommodation. Frequent rally attenders have such facilities. The next picture shows how entry is gained.

This picture shows the living accommodation of the previous picture. These are usually fitted out caravan style, with all facilities.

A 1949 Austin K2 two-axle flat truck. In 1939 Austin were only making cars. They then received a state order to build trucks. Called series one, there were two models, K2 and K3, carrying two and three tons respectively and fitted with a four-litre petrol engine. Post-war models such as this received an updated radiator grille. Also known as a Birmingham Bedford, due to similarity in looks.

An action shot showing a tender unloading a Ford Thames Trader at Birch with extreme exhaust emissions.

Here is a 1966 Ford Thames Trader series two, seen in the livery of Tim Speight of Boroughbridge, North Yorkshire. A short wheelbase fitted with a rugged steel tipping body, frequently seen on building sites and motorway construction projects.

This is a further action shot showing delivery of a vehicle entered on the run. It is not uncommon for vehicles such as this Atkinson, hailing from Market Drayton, to be transported to the start, in this case Birch, and for the tender to follow to the finish. At the end of the event, the vehicle is then returned back to base.

A 1947 Atkinson FC1407 three-axle truck. Fitted with a drop-side body, it is in the livery of Malcom Harrison's Auctions, Market Drayton and fitted with an AEC 7.7-litre petrol engine. British Road Services were big buyers of this type of vehicle.

This is a 1959 AEC Mammoth Major mark two built as a six-compartment tanker, new to Shell Mex and BP and bought by its present owner as a Chinese six: two front axles and one rear. In restoration it was returned to four axles, with major cab work, two new front wings and a new aluminium tank fitted.

A 1958 Commer Superpoise B mark four, it was new to Nottinghamshire Fire Brigade as a foam and salvage tender. Registration numbers 999 were frequently allocated to emergency service vehicles when first registered. This vehicle was accident damaged in 1984 and stored for 21 years before restoration and conversion into a lorry.

Roy Dodsworth collectior

A 1952 Atkinson TS1066 twin-steer flatbed truck, in the livery of Malcolm Harrison of Nantwich. Another example of a two-steering-axle vehicle, rarely seen in preservation, referred to as a 'Chinese six'. This vehicle is a regular attender at local events in the North, and seen on previous occasions carrying a Fordson tractor.

An extremely rare vehicle in preservation. This is a Crossley 25/30 light tender issued to the Royal Flying Corps in WW1. It is canvas covered and fitted with double tyres on the rear wheels, with two spare tyres affixed to the driver's door. Note the starting handle to the front.

This is a War Department 1941 Austin K2 fire engine, in NFS (National Fire Service) grey. It is fitted out with firefighting equipment, and with seating accommodation for four operatives. It has an extending ladder and water hoses to both sides. The headlights are covered in accordance with wartime regulations so as not to be visible from the air, thwarting any attack from enemy aircraft. Over 13,000 emergency service vehicles were built by Austin from 1940 to the end of the war.

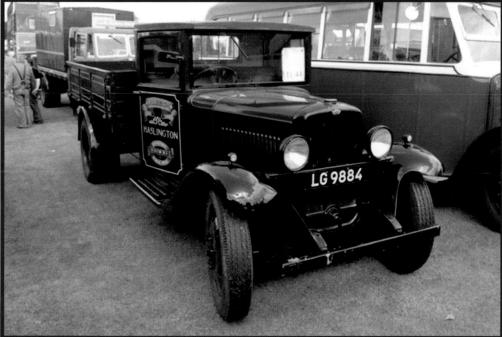

A rare survivor from the Bedford production line of WHG/WLG models which were made from 1931 to 1935. It is virtually indistinguishable from a Chevrolet LG, its predecessor, apart from the radiator grille badging. This is a 1932 model and owned by J. Leech, who is a collector of classic vehicles, regularly supporting events in the UK.

This is a Noddy van. BRS Parcels Division were looking for an ideal delivery van and such a vehicle was developed by NFC, the owners of BRS. Austin VA chassis were chosen, and Star Bodies, the inhouse bodybuilder of NFC, built large numbers from 1958 to the 1970s. Fleet number of the van illustrated is 34NW983. I have been unable to trace the reason they were called 'Noddy' vans.

This vehicle is very rare and interesting. A 1914 American La France Torpedo firefighting appliance, fitted with a hose bed of two-inch firefighting hose for use with two chemical tanks. Seen at Birch in 2009 when the vehicle was entered by Robert Preston from Goole.

A 1956 Leyland Comet 90 mark one two-axle flat wagon. It has a sheeted load and is in the livery of Simpson Bros of Stocksfield-on-Tyne. The Comet name was carried forward as and when new models were developed.

Roy Dodsworth collection 2010

A 1967 Leyland Octopus four-axle flat lorry, fitted with an ERGO cab also found on AEC and Albion trucks. All Octopus models are eight-wheelers, and this is in the livery of Malcolm Harrison, a specialist used-truck specialist of Stone in Staffordshire. Martin has a number of classic trucks and attends many rallies in the season.

Roy Dodsworth collection 2010

Here is a 1952 Austin K9 4x4 British heavy military truck, built by Austin when an independent manufacturer. Large numbers were sold to the military authorities. It is unusual in that it had a constant mesh (crash) box and a cable handbrake, and looks very smart in civilian 'attire'. Sometimes vehicles are difficult to photograph, as in this instance, due to areas being cordoned off to facilitate parking.

UFF 901

A 1976 Atkinson Borderer two-axle tractor unit coupled to a two-axle twin-wheeled bulk canvas arched tipper. It is fitted with a Rolls-Royce engine and is in the livery of Steve Parr Haulage. The previous owner was V. G. Mathers, a Scottish haulier.

ROY DODSWORTH COLLECTION 2011

A 1969 AEC Mercury two-axle flatbed truck carrying possible living/catering accommodation. Fitted with an ERGO cab, this truck attends many rallies in the North and Midlands. The restoration is visually first class although no information is available.

A 1954 Seddon T5 two-axle flatbed lorry in the livery of William Hunter and part of the Hunter Collection of preserved vehicles. The radiator bears the insignia of Perkins, indicating that one of their diesel engines is fitted. Above the cab roof is a headboard used for carrying folded load sheets. Seen driven by Glyn Owen, a longtime driver for the Hunter Collection.

The biggest vehicle in the book is this 1976 three-axle Scammell Contractor tractor unit, named Renown, which was fleet number 600 in the fleets of Wynns Heavy Haulage. It bears STGO Cat 3 plating for work with heavy or abnormal loads. It averages six miles per gallon.

Roy Dodsworth coll

The Scammell Contractor on arrival at Harrogate on a low-loader prior to unloading.

A further picture of the Scammell Contractor. Having managed to climb into the cab, I got quite a good view of the road ahead.

Roy Dodsworth collection 2014

This is a 1936 International four-ton drop-side truck which was sent in kit form from the USA and assembled at International Tractors plant at Doncaster. It was bought new by a farmer in Barton on Humber, from Peacock & Binnington, International Tractor dealers of Brigg, and was used mainly at harvest time. It is in the livery of, and still owned by, Osgerbys' Haulage, also of Barton on Humber, who are the second owners of the vehicle. It had a restoration in the early 1970s and was entered in the Trans Pennine Run for a number of years. It has a six-cylinder side-valve petrol engine, and has rack and pinion steering. The tipping body is hand wound. Picture, taken at Mytholmroyd in 1982, courtesy of Charlotte Else.

This is a 1927 four-ton Dennis lorry, the chassis of which was supplied new to London builders Higgs & Hill Ltd. The body was built in the company's own workshops and was ready for use in late 1927. It was sold for £35 in 1942, having travelled in excess of 250,000 miles, to Smith Clayton Forge in Lincoln. In the late 1960s it was acquired by Lincolnshire Vintage Vehicle Society, in whose ownership it remains. The truck is seen at Mytholmroyd in 1982 on its way to Harrogate. Picture courtesy of Charlotte Else.

This is a 1931 Dodge 30 cwt flat truck which started life with a wholesale grocer in Biddulph, Staffordshire, and was later sold to a farmer for carrying farm produce and manure. Bought by North Cheshire Motors in 1963 and restored by them, it was seen on the HCVS London to Brighton Run in 1971, having been entered by G. B. Ward of Warrington. This picture was taken on the 1982 Trans Pennine Run and is seen at Mytholmroyd. Picture courtesy of Charlotte Else.

Now the end of the day and 200+ vehicles will be leaving the site. Some owners will have won prizes, and along with all other entrants, hopefully will have enjoyed the day, with lots of chatter and gossip! Lots of work still to do and volunteers will be tidying up, emptying the bins and returning the site back to normal. A big thankyou to everyone taking part. I hope you have enjoyed reading this book and my grateful thanks to the publishing team at Old Pond Publishers for making it happen!